INDOOR PLANTS:
keeping them alive and well

by Victor Minot

W. Foulsham & Co. Ltd.

London · New York · Toronto · Cape Town · Sydney

W. Foulsham & Company Limited
Yeovill Road, Slough, Berkshire, SL1 4JH

ISBN 0-572-01236-5

Plants for photographs on pages 26, 40, 52, 74, 92 and
cover courtesy of L.R. Russell Ltd., Windelsham and
W. Wood and Son Ltd., Taplow.

First published by Foulsham in hardback 1981

Printed in Hong Kong

Looking after your plants

Anyone can grow indoor plants successfully if they abide by a few simple rules and remember that the most important thing is to identify the plant's needs and cater to them as much as possible.

Location
All plants require certain essentials — such as light and water — to keep them alive and well, and obviously different plants require slightly different conditions. So the first thing to decide is where to position a plant where the conditions suit that plant's particular needs. Will it manage to thrive, for example, on an east-facing window sill above a radiator, or will it need to be on a main window sill where it is light and draught-free without strong direct sunlight?

Grouping
Grouping plants together can be very effective if the subjects are carefully chosen. They must not only complement each other in appearance, however, but must flourish in similar conditions of light, temperature and humidity otherwise a successful group of plants will be spoilt by one or two which are not suited to the conditions.

Light
Plants use the energy in light to produce food by the process known as photosynthesis. The lower the light level, the less food is made, so it is wise to give them all the light you can make available.

Warmth
Few indoor plants will tolerate more than 22°C (70°). Too high a temperature will result in excessive evaporation from the plant and the leaves will dry out.
Never leave plants in full sunlight, otherwise they

will quickly dry out, suffering scorched leaves, flowers, and also roots if the soil surface is exposed and baked.

Plants object to sudden temperature fluctuations, so draughts should always be avoided. Never leave plants on a window sill after drawing the curtains in cold weather, as this creates a damaging frost pocket.

Air
Plants need fresh air, and the air around them should circulate freely to help remove traces of gas or other toxic fumes. Remember, however, that ventilation and fresh air do not mean draughts, which are harmful even to sturdy plants.

Dust
Dust is a plant enemy which makes the foliage look dull, blocks leaf pores and inhibits the plant's respiration. Remove dust by spraying and gently sponging the leaves with clean water, avoiding the smallest, new leaves in case of damage.

Water
Water is essential to plants — overwatering is the most common cause of the death of house plants, so assess your plant's individual needs and do not just water according to rigid rules. Succulents need less water than thinner-leaved plants; in winter when a plant is less active, it needs less water than when the temperature and light are increased and growth is stimulated.

If possible, use rainwater to water your plants as it is chemically neutral. Tap water contains several chemicals, particularly lime, which can damage plants, so if you use tap water, boil it then leave it to cool before using it on your indoor plants. Most of the lime will then be deposited in the kettle. Never use very cold water, but always tepid water.

Every day, assess the soil condition of each plant and provide the right amount of water. The right soil condition for each plant is described under their individual entries. Press the soil with your thumb. Wet soil feels soggy and lifeless; the thumb makes a mark which remains. Moist soil will feel springy and the thumb mark will disappear. Particles of soil will stick to the thumb in both cases. Dry soil feels dry and firm, often hard. It will not give to thumb pressure and few, if any, particles will stick to your thumb.

Humidity
Most plants need a humid atmosphere. The exception is the cacti, which have developed means of countering the hostile conditions of their native habitat.

Occasional spraying satisfies the needs of most plants. Use a hand sprayer which produces a very fine spray, almost a mist, so that no droplets collect on leaves and damage them. Spray in the morning so that the plants are dry by nightfall.

For plants which require high humidity, half fill a large plant saucer with pebbles. Push into them a smaller inverted saucer and stand the plant on this. Add water to a level slightly below the base of the plant pot. Replace evaporation loss as necessary.

Feeding
All plants need nitrogen for growth and good foliage; phosphorus for strong root systems; potassium for good flowers and fruit; plus trace elements. Use a compound fertiliser for indoor plants. Feed when the soil is in the right condition (see individual entries) and in the growing season. Never overfeed as this will damage and may kill the plant.

Pests and diseases
Systemic fungicides are available to spray indoor plants to prevent infection. If plants are attacked, early discovery and treatment are essential. When it is necessary to remove a leaf, stem or flower which will leave a moist open would, spray the cut with flowers of sulphur to inhibit fungal disease. Always use a sterilised compost, never unsterilised garden soil.

Rot is most often caused by overwatering, especially in winter. A plant with root rot will die. To control, always use sterilised compost. Keep the plant warm and do not overwater. Spray with fungicide.

Mildew (botrytis) is the result of a stagnant, humid atmosphere, and looks like grey mould on stems and leaves. Improve conditions and ensure good ventilation. Spray with fungicide.

Blackfly, whitefly or greenfly breed on new shoots and under leaves and exude a sticky honey dew. Spray with greenfly killer.

Red spider mites attack the underside of leaves. The leaves become brittle and the plant weak. Spray with liquid derris every two days.

Scale insects are waxy shells found on stems and leaves of shrubby plants. Growth is weakened and the plant is sticky. *Mealy bugs* are small pests with a white, cottony covering found on the undersides of leaves in summer. Use a matchstick tipped with cotton wool soaked in methylated spirit to rub them from the plant.

Thrips are tiny, black, winged insects which attack leaves and flowers, leaving white marks. Growth is stunted. Spray with Malathion or Topguard dust.

Pots, compost and re-potting

Always choose the correct size pot for the plant. The best compost to use is a proprietary loam-free compost designed for house plants.

Never re-pot a plant unless it is pot-bound. You can tell this if the plant grows slowly even if adequately fed; the compost dries out quickly; and plant roots hang from the drainage hole. As a final check, allow the compost to become slightly dry. Spread the fingers of one hand across the top of the pot, turn the pot upside down, tap the pot gently, and lift off the pot. In a pot-bound plant, a mass of roots will wind around the outside of the pot.

If the plant needs re-potting, choose a pot just slightly larger. Cover the drainage holes with crocks then a layer of compost. Take the plant out of its present pot, remove the old crocks and stand in the new pot, then gradually fill the space with fresh, damp potting compost. Firm down the compost as you go. Water carefully and place in slight shade for about a week before returning to its normal place.

Pruning

Pinching out can improve the shape of plant or encourage growth in a different direction. Pinching out is done by pulling the growing tip steadily backwards so that it snaps off at a leaf joint. If the plant is not brittle, then the growing tip must be cut out by pinching it between your thumb nail and forefinger. Once the growing tip has been removed, both the tiny buds at the leaf joints will begin to grow. This will encourage a bushy shape.

For plants which bear flowers on the new season's growth, such as fuchsia, prune back severely when flowering is over. Cut cleanly across the stem just above a bud. never prune plants which flower on the growth of the previous season or you will remove all the next season's flowers.

Always cut out dead or diseased stems.

Individual plants

The following pages contain advice on looking after individual plants. In addition to the general information, each plant has been given a 'daisy rating' indicating whether it is ideal for the beginner, or a subject which needs more care and attention.

 Easy plants which will stand up to quite a lot of mistreatment.

 Also easy to grow; should present no problems provided they are given reasonable consideration.

 These will thrive if the instruction on their care are followed.

Saintpaulia ionantha

AFRICAN VIOLET

A low-growing plant with dark green, hairy leaves growing in a circle around its centre. Clusters of vivid flowers occupy the centre of the plant when it is in bloom. It will flower for several months given reasonable care. There are varieties in white, red, purple or pink and others with double blossoms. The most popularly sold are of the single purple variety.

Temperatures:

Growing season	15–22 °C	(60–72 °F)
Minimum winter	13 °C	(50 °F)

Soil: A soil-less compost.

Where it likes to be: In a light position out of full sun, except in winter when some sunlight is appreciated. They dislike draughts and sudden temperature changes.

What it likes to drink: Use tepid soft water introduced below the leaves, straight onto the soil. Do not splash; droplets mark the leaves and cause holes. Water must not get into the crown of the plant; it remains and causes rotting. The plant needs high humidity; see page 5. Mist spray daily in hot weather, weekly at other times.

Making it sensational: Snip off faded flowers and damaged leaves. Avoid sun damage. Re-pot it when necessary; too large a pot results in lush soft growth and fewer flowers. Give very weak liquid fertilizer fortnightly.

Giving it a rest: After flowering, it takes a short rest but this is more beneficial if extended by reducing water gradually until the soil is kept just moist for six weeks. Annual re-potting is essential in a wide shallow pot so that the leaves rest on its rim. Then gradually increase watering and in summer feed the plant.

When it looks sick:
Spotted, unsightly leaves: Caused by water droplets remaining on the leaves. Always shake them off.
The plant looks dull and dry: Check that soil condition is correct. If it is, move the plant to an East-facing window away from bright sunlight. Mist-spray regularly.
Mealy bugs : If found—see page 6.

Pilea cadieri

ALUMINIUM PLANT

A quickly growing plant, with decorative leaves distinctively marked in silver, it mixes well with other foliage plants and is a suitable subject for planting in an indoor garden or trough. It is also called Artillery Plant because it ejects pollen when a plant in flower is sprayed.

Temperatures:

Growing season	20-24°C	(69-75°F)
Minimum winter	10°C	(50°F)

Soil: A soil-less compost.

Where it likes to be: In good light or in semi-shaded conditions, protected from summer sun and draughts.

What it likes to drink: In summer, water to maintain a moist soil condition. In winter, it should be less springy to thumb pressure, though particles adhere. Avoid splashing the leaves; water stains them. It likes high humidity; see page 5.

Making it sensational: Give weak liquid feed weekly while growing. Pinch out growing tips to force it to branch and produce a good bushy shape. If you do not, the plant grows leggy and ungainly.

Giving it a rest: It rests in winter. As growth ceases, reduce water and stop feeding. Re-pot in spring. Cut back stems to half their height and maintain a moist soil condition. Six weeks after re-growth begins, resume feeding.

When it looks sick:
Poor colouring : This results from insufficient light. Improve the light but do not place the plant in direct sunlight.
Dry, dusty-looking leaves, lacking a healthy sheen : Inadequate humidity will cause this. Improve the humidity and mist-spray regularly.
Stained blotchy leaves : Caused by water splashes. Always shake them off.
Poor growth and yellowing foliage : Water the plant with $\frac{1}{4}$ oz magnesium sulphate (Epsom Salts) to 1 pint of water—30 gm to 1 litre.

Asparagus setaceus

ASPARAGUS FERN

An extremely graceful plant with fine feathery foliage which arches from the top of slender, erect stems. It combines superbly with other foliage plants and is undemanding.

Temperatures:

Growing season	18 °C	(64 °F)
Minimum winter	8–10 °C	(46–50 °F)

Soil: A soil-less compost or John Innes No 2.

Where it likes to be: Is not demanding of light but if too shaded will grow towards the light. Draughts if severe, will cause foliage to lose tiny leaflets.

What it likes to drink: Keep soil well moistened during growing season. Feed with weak liquid fertilizer once monthly.

Making it sensational: This is not a troublesome plant but if it does become unsightly a cut back in the autumn will result in renewed growth from the bottom after the rest period.

Giving it a rest: In winter, reduce water drastically. Place in frost-free position. To re-start in spring, gradually increase watering. As new fronds appear, resume feeding.

When it looks sick:
Browning, dying fronds: Clip out the dying stems and place the plant in a more shaded situation.
The entire plant begins to brown and the leaves begin to drop their tiny leaflets: This is due to over-watering or waterlogging of the soil. Re-pot the plant carefully in fresh soil. The plant will be checked but is likely to recover.

Azalea Indica

AZALEA, INDIAN

A beautiful dwarf shrub, usually of good shape with slightly domed top. Very colourful when in flower, since almost the entire plant is covered in blooms, it is available in a number of different shades of red or pink, and also in white, making a brilliant splash of colour. The flowers appear before the foliage matures—the early, pale green leaves enlarge to about $1\frac{1}{2}$ in long, becoming dark green and slightly glossy.

Temperatures:

Growing season	15-24°C	(60-75°F)
Minimum	12°C	(53°F)

Soil: A lime-free compost with good drainage.

Where it likes to be: Keep in a well lit, airy place, away from direct sunlight. Keep out of draughts.

What it likes to drink: Use rainwater or soft water, never <u>tap</u> water. Maintain moist soil condition; it should never dry out. The plant needs high humidity from the time the buds form right through the flowering period (see page 5). Mist-spray the buds daily with tepid soft water. If they become dry they will drop off.

Making it sensational: Careful watering and cool steady temperatures. Green shoots beside flower buds should be pulled back until they snap off, to avoid sapping the strength of the buds. Feed well-diluted liquid fertilizer weekly. Pinch off dead flowers.

Giving it a rest: The shoots which appear after flowering finishes must be allowed to grow, as next year's flower buds will form at their tips. Re-pot if necessary. Keep the plant, well watered, in a cool room, or a shady spot in the garden from early summer until early autumn.

When it looks sick:
Leaves fall: Place plant in cooler spot.
Leaves become yellow: Tap water may have been used. They are lime-haters and must have soft water.
Buds drop: Place plant in cool spot away from draughts. Mist-spray with tepid water.
Plant looks dull and dry: Water regularly to maintain a moist soil condition. Good drainage is a <u>must</u>.
Pale yellowing leaves: Add a pinch of sequestrene of iron to its next watering.

Begonia lucerna

BEGONIA

An attractive plant with a great number of varieties. The leaves are narrow 'Angel Wings', often red-veined. The flowers, usually coral, though other colours can be obtained, are borne in fine, pendulous trusses.

Temperatures:

Growing season	15–22 °C	(60–72 °F)
Minimum winter	13 °C	(55 °F)

Soil: 70 % soil-less or John Innes No 2 compost mixed with 30 % peat.

Where it likes to be: Will accept good light or light shade, but needs protection from strong sunlight. It is not very sensitive to draughts or <u>moderate</u> temperature changes.

What it likes to drink: Lukewarm rain water or soft water. Maintain a moist, springy soil condition. Ensure good drainage. Mist-spray plants in hot weather, but avoid allowing droplets to collect on leaves. Provide humidity by a method from page 5.

Making it sensational: Feed weekly with a weak liquid fertilizer. Remove the dead blooms and lower leaves if they become damaged or unsightly. Do not pinch out shoots.

Giving it a rest: Reduce water to maintain moist soil condition and stop feeding. As growth becomes vigorous, increase warmth and provide a little more water. Begin feeding again after one month.

When it looks sick:
Plant flags: Reduce water until soil condition is springy. Check drainage.
Dried brown areas on the leaves: Caused by under-watering or draughts or severe temperature changes. All are simple to rectify and should be done at once.
Buds drop: This is likely from all causes, i.e. over or under-watering, draughts, temperature changes. All must be checked and rectified.
Fungus: May attack open wounds. Dust with fungicidal powder.

Begonia Rex

BEGONIA

A medium sized, usually well-shaped foliage plant.
The large leaves are beautifully coloured with a silver
band running parallel to the leaf's edge. They are
mostly used to provide contrast with other plants
kept in their company.

Temperatures:

Growing season	15–22 °C	(60–72 °F)
Minimum winter	13 °C	(55 °F)

Soil: A mixture of 30% peat and 70% soil-less compost.

18

Where it likes to be: It thrives in good light or semi-shade, and tolerates draughts and temperature changes. Keep out of strong sunlight.

What it likes to drink: Lukewarm water. Maintain a moist springy soil condition; do not allow the soil to dry out. Mist-spray weekly—droplets must not form on the leaves. This plant likes humidity; use a method from page 5.

Making it sensational: Give well-diluted liquid fertilizer weekly during the growing season. Remove any dead leaves close to the main stem and dust the wound lightly with fungicide powder. Pinch out the flowers as they appear. Only pinch out shoots to produce a good shape.

Giving it a rest: Growth slows in winter. Give less water and stop feeding. Rest for six weeks, then increase light and warmth. As growth starts, increase water to maintain the correct soil condition. Feed when growth becomes vigorous.

When it looks sick:
Plant flags: Stop watering until the soil condition is springy to the touch.
Dry brown areas on leaves: Restore soil condition and water regularly to retain it.
Browning leaf edges: Ensure that the plant is not suffering from draughts or temperature fluctuations.
Fungus: May establish itself on open wounds; use a fungicidal dusting powder.

Impatiens sultani

BUSY LIZZIE, BALSAM

Vigorous and easy to grow, these free-flowering plants are very popular, and ideal for children to grow. The leaves are light green and attractive, and the prolific flowers may be red, pink, salmon or white. This plant is very tolerant and will accept a wide range of conditions.

Temperatures:

Growing season	15-22°C	(60-72°F)
Minimum winter	12°C	(53°F)

Soil: A soil-less or John Innes No 2 compost.

Where it likes to be: In good light protected from strong sunlight.

What it likes to drink: Maintain a moist soil condition; do not let it dry out. In summer it grows rapidly and needs frequent watering. Mist-spray daily during warm weather. If the leaves droop, the humidity must be increased.

Making it sensational: 'Pinch out' when it is young to encourage a good shape and then stop. Remove faded flowers. As it grows, staking is advisable; the stems are brittle and may snap under their own weight. Give a weak liquid fertilizer weekly.

Giving it a rest: In winter, keep in a warm, light place and water sparingly, keeping soil just moist. Feed while flowering continues. These plants become unsightly with age. Discard and propagate new ones. Cuttings made below a leaf joint will root easily, even in water.

When it looks sick:
Leaves yellow and drop: This can result from over-watering or bad drainage. Reduce water and watch to see if the water sinks quickly through the soil. If it does not—re-pot with special attention to drainage.
The plant tends to wilt: It is a vigorous grower and probably needs repotting.
The plant becomes leggy and ungainly: Cut back unsightly stems at a leaf joint. Dust cuts with fungicide powder. Pinch out tips to make it bushy.

Citrus mitis

CALAMONDIN ORANGE

This attractive miniature orange tree originates from the Philippines and is becoming increasingly popular. The plant bears scented white flowers at the same time as the colourful fruits. The fruits are edible, although a little bitter. The leaves are very dark green and shiny.

Temperatures:
Growing season	15-18°C	(60-65°F)
Minimum winter	10°C	(50°F)

Soil: A soil-less compost. Good drainage is essential.

Where it likes to be: Find a position near a window with plenty of light and fresh air but no draughts. These plants do best if placed outdoors in bright light in summer.

What it likes to drink: Use tap water. Water frequently to ensure a moist soil but do not allow to become waterlogged. Spray every day.

Making it sensational: Feed every fourteen days in summer. If kept outside during the summer months, the flowers will be insect-pollinated, but if grown indoors, pollinate with a brush.

Giving it a rest: Keep in a moderately warm, light position during the winter when growth slows. Water occasionally to prevent the compost drying out.

When it looks sick:
Leaves turn pale: The plant needs feeding.
Leaves fall: Either too hot and dry, or the plant has been overwatered. Test the soil, then either water and spray or leave to dry out.
Plant growth tall and thin: The plant will grow bushier in a cooler, better ventilated position.
The plant does not flower: Move to a lighter place.
Insect pests: Identify from page 6 and treat as instructed.
Leaves curl and turn brown: The plant is in a draught. Find a more sheltered position.

Calathea makoyana

CALATHEA

An attractive foliage plant. The large oval leaves are matt green, with distinctive brown bars superimposed upon a creamy white ground. It resembles the Prayer Plant (Maranta) but is hardier and somewhat larger.

Temperatures:
Growing season	15-20°C	(60-69°F)
Minimum winter	10°C	(50°F)

Soil: A soil-less compost.

Where it likes to be: It likes plenty of light. It will tolerate shade but not direct sunlight. It will resent draughts or extreme temperature fluctuation.

What it likes to drink: Keep soil moist and provide humidity. Mist-spray twice weekly and feed with weak liquid fertilizer once a week.

Making it sensational: Cut out unsightly leaves, using a slanted cut, and lightly dust with fungicide powder. The plant looks better and is happier in a container with other taller foliage plants.

Giving it a rest: Reduce watering and cease feeding in winter.

When it looks sick:
The plant looks unkempt and dull: Bad drainage or over-watering are suspect and should be corrected. Withhold water for a while. If the soil is waterlogged it may be best to re-pot.
Dry leaves with browning tips or edges: Increase humidity. Mist-spray regularly.
Unsightly leaves with brown edges: See under 'Making it sensational'.
Scale insects: See page 6 for treatment.

Streptocarpus

CAPE PRIMROSE

Streptocarpus hybrids are available in a range of
colours from white through pink to mauve. They are
pretty plants with long, bright green oval leaves like
those of the primula. The dainty flowers are carried
in clusters at the tops of slender stems, of which
there may be quite a number on a well grown plant.

Temperatures:

Growing season	12–22 °C	(53–70 °F)
Minimum winter	12°C	(53 °F)

Soil: A soil-less compost.

Where it likes to be: In good light in winter; never in full sun. It dislikes draughts and temperature changes. Ample humidity is needed.

What it likes to drink: Keep soil moist to thumb pressure. Never allow to dry out as the leaves will flag badly and may be damaged. Mist-spray regularly, except in winter.

Making it sensational: Give very weak liquid fertilizer weekly in growing season. Stop when plant begins to flower. Remove faded flowers and stems.

Giving it a rest: Reduce water but do not allow foliage to die down. Maintain minimum temperature of 12 °C (53 °F). Re-pot in spring with soil-less compost.

When it looks sick:
Flagging leaves, lacking their usual gloss: Check the soil condition; if dry, water and use a fine spray on the leaves. If the soil is moist, spray only and improve the humidity—see page 5. Keep out of strong sunlight.
Leaves pale and become dull: Aphids—see page 6.
Mildew on damaged leaves: Dust with a fungicidal powder.

Zygocactus truncatus,
Shlumbergera Russeliana
CHRISTMAS CACTUS, EASTER CACTUS

These are the easiest to grow of all leafy cacti, and
are remarkably floriferous. The leaves form part of
a segmented stem. Both these plants come from
Brazil. *Zygocactus* is the true Christmas cactus;
Shlumbergera flowers a month or two later and is
known as the Easter cactus. They can be obtained
with flowers of delicate shades of white, pink, and
flamingo reds and oranges. They are highly useful
for providing colour in mid-winter and early spring.

Temperatures:

Growing season	22–24 °C	(72–75 °F)
Minimum winter	10 °C	(50 °F)

Soil: Soil-less compost to which 10% sand has been
added.

Where it likes to be: It needs plenty of light but should be protected from hot sun. It likes a fairly even temperature.

What it likes to drink: Use lukewarm water to keep the soil just moist to thumb pressure until the buds form; then increase the amount slightly as the buds swell, avoiding the leaves. Excessive watering causes buds to drop. Never spray.

Making it sensational: Feed very occasionally with liquid fertilizer heavily diluted. It must be kept in the same position and never handled or moved. Carefully twist off dead blooms.

Giving it a rest: It rests when flowering is over. Reduce water. After six weeks, re-pot into compost with a little sandy grit added. Do not use too big a pot; this stimulates leaf growth and reduces the flowers.

When it looks sick:
The leaves assume a corrugated appearance: This is the effect of under-watering. Water the plant but avoid over-watering.
The flower buds drop: This happens if the plant is moved or rotated after the buds have formed. Cease feeding at this point.
Pale sickly looking leaves result from over-feeding: Stop feed and water with soft water.
Mealy bugs : Deal with them as shown on page 6.

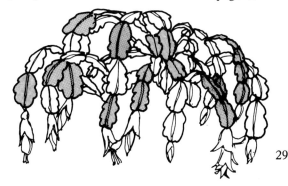

29

Senecio

CINERARIA

Still widely known, incorrectly, as Cineraria. It is a large-leaved plant with brilliant daisy-like flowers borne in dense heads during winter and spring. The colours cover a very wide range; blue with white centres are the most commonly seen.

Temperature:
Minimum, growing season   12 °C   (53 °F)

Soil: A soil-less or John Innes No 2 compost.

Where it likes to be: A cool light position out of full sun. It objects to draughts which make leaves go limp.

What it likes to drink: Keep soil moist—never let it dry out. It likes some humidity and in dry weather, mist-spray the leaves. This prevents excessive respiration and stops leaves from wilting.

Making it sensational: They are usually bought in flower and feeding is unnecessary. If kept in cool conditions they last very well.

Giving it a rest: They can be over-wintered but are not worth the trouble as they are quite cheap and second year plants seldom equal new young specimens.

When it looks sick:
Flagging leaves hanging limply over the sides of the pot: Check soil condition; if dry, water. Give the leaves a fine spray. If the soil is moist, spray only and move into light shade to recover.
Erect, lack-lustre leaves probably with a blotchy appearance: Possibly aphids—see page 6.
The mildewy growth of fungus: Dust promptly with a fungicidal powder.

Zebrina pendula

COMMELINAS

Zebrina pendula is a very popular plant often mistaken for a Tradescantia which has similar form and growth habit. The variety 'Quadricolor' has green, purple and white-striped leaves, whose crystalline shimmer makes them most attractive. It trails well and is fine kept in a fairly high position. This is one of the least demanding plants. It mixes well with other indoor foliage plants.

Temperatures:

Growing season	12-22°C	(53-72°F)
Minimum winter	7°C	(45°F)

Soil: A mixture of soil-less compost and 20% good friable garden loam.

Where it likes to be: In good light which promotes good colour. It tolerates shade, draughts and varying temperatures. Avoid hot sunlight.

What it likes to drink: Tepid water. Maintain a moist soil condition. It needs no regular spraying but mist-spraying occasionally. No special humidity required.

Making it sensational: Give a weak liquid fertilizer monthly. Trim the stems to keep it tidy and attractive.

Giving it a rest: It grows continuously. There is no marked resting period but less water is needed in winter to maintain the correct soil condition.

When it looks sick:
The distance between leaves on the same stem is long: The plant is becoming 'drawn'; give it more light.
Leaves die, becoming brown, dry and brittle: The plant is grossly under-watered. Plunge the plant in tepid water to wetten the soil ball. Then drain.
The leaf colour becomes glossy green instead of retaining its purple striping: This is a symptom of inadequate light.

Cordyline terminalis

CORDYLINE

The Cordyline is a showy foliage plant. It has long, flat leaves variegated in green and cream with red veins. It cannot be described as an easy plant to keep. It needs some space and is not always suitable for grouping with other plants.

Temperatures:

Growing season	15-22°C	(60-72°F)
Minimum winter	13°C	(55°F)

Soil: A soil-less compost.

Where it likes to be: A good light position, not in direct sunlight. It dislikes draughts and temperature changes.

What it likes to drink: Tepid rainwater to maintain a moist springy soil condition; good drainage is important. Always water on the soil. Mist-spray daily and gently sponge the leaves if they appear dusty or dull. The plant likes high humidity—see page 5.

Making it sensational: Feed weekly with weak liquid fertilizer. No stopping or pruning needed but re-pot when the plant becomes cramped.

Giving it a rest: There is no marked rest period. Growth will slow in colder weather. Maintain soil moisture and stop feeding until warmer weather speeds up growth.

When it looks sick:
Plant loses lower leaves: The humidity is insufficient.
The plant flags: This can result from over- or under-watering or poor drainage. Check the soil condition. Ensure good drainage.
The plant pales and tends to flag: Stop feeding. Ensure that it is not subjected to draughts or temperature changes.
Plant looks tired and dull: Mist-spray regularly and sponge the leaves gently.

Codiaeum variegatum

CROTON

Both leaf shape and colour can vary considerably in this attractive plant, but all have strong yellow or orange splashes of colour on elongated leaves. They thrive in a very bright position, away from draughts.

Temperatures:

Growing season	15-27°C	(60-80°F)
Minimum	13°C	(55°F)

Soil: A soil-less compost.

Where it likes to be: In a position to get as much light as possible. They can be placed in direct sunlight. Avoid fluctuations in temperature, and draughts.

What it likes to drink: Tepid water. Keep the soil moist and springy and never let the plant dry out. Spray daily in summer, but not while in direct sunlight.

Making it sensational: The leaf colour will improve the more light is available, so position the plant carefully. Feed regularly during the growing season, about every two weeks. Avoid changes in temperature.

Giving it a rest: Growth slows in winter. Keep the soil just moist.

When it looks sick:
The plant looses its leaves: Either too dry, too cold or an uneven temperature. Move to a warmer place and spray regularly.
Insect pests : Identify from page 6 and treat as instructed.
Leaves dull and loose colour variation: Needs more light. Move to a better position.
Leaves scorched: Caused by spraying in direct sunlight.
Leaves droop: Too wet. Allow to dry out then water less frequently.

Cyclamen persicum, Cyclamen latifolium

CYCLAMEN

These tuberous plants came from Asia Minor. They
have dainty flowers in white, pink, crimson, cerise,
salmon or scarlet, carried on slender straight stems.
Most are very vividly coloured, even on dull winter
days. The heart-shaped leaves are attractively mar-
bled. There are both miniature and larger forms, all
capable of surviving several years with proper care.
It is better to buy a plant in bud in order to enjoy
the display longer.

Temperatures:
Growing season	12-20°C	(60-72°F)
Minimum winter	10°C	(50°F)

Soil: A soil-less compost.

Where it likes to be: In good light, but not direct sunlight. Although this plant is fairly tolerant, draughts and temperature changes will make it unkempt and unhappy looking.

What it likes to drink: Lukewarm water—cold water could be fatal. Always ensure that the soil is moist and springy to thumb pressure, but not soggy. Do not allow water to remain in the plant saucer. It likes humidity; see page 5. Give an occasional mist-spray in hot weather and shade the plant from sunlight. Do not over-spray; the top of the corm must not be wetted.

Making it sensational: Feeding once or twice per season with very weak liquid fertilizer is ample; never feed when in bud or in flower. Always remove faded flowers to allow other buds to develop.

Giving it a rest: Rest when flowering ends. Reduce watering during this period but keep soil slightly moist.

When it looks sick:
The leaf stems droop and lie down: The plant needs watering. Use lukewarm water in several doses to avoid wetting the corm. Recovery is usually swift.
A poor specimen: This may be due to an old, corky tuber and cannot be corrected. Always remove faded flowers to allow the development of more buds.
Sickly plant : Check for parasites—see page 6.

Dracaena

DRAGON TREE

There are many varieties of this tall, palm-like plant. Both leaf shape and colour can vary considerably, but the most popular have green and red, or green and yellow leaves. All are variegated. They are quite easy to care for, and do well grouped with other plants.

Temperatures:

Growing season	18-24°C	(65-75°F)
Minimum winter	13°C	(55°F)

Soil: A soil-less compost.

Where it likes to be: Plenty of light maintains the colour variation in the leaves, but avoid direct sunlight. Avoid draughts.

What it likes to drink: Keep the soil moist but avoid over-watering. Never let the soil dry out. Spray twice weekly in summer.

Making it sensational: Feed every fourteen days and keep in a light position.

Giving it a rest: Growth slows in winter, so water occasionally to keep the compost just moist, allowing the top layer to dry out between waterings.

When it looks sick:
Plant looses its leaves: Needs watering and spraying as conditions are too dry and hot.
Insect pests : Identify from page 6 and treat as instructed.
Growth stops and leaves fall: The temperature is too low. Move to a warmer place.
Plant droops and rots: Over-watering. Allow to dry out then water less frequently.

Dieffenbachia

DUMB CANE

A striking foliage plant with large elongated oval leaves which are bright green with blotches and spots of yellow. The sap is poisonous and if chewed will cause pain and numbness of the tongue (hence the name). It should be kept away from children or pets. It is not easy to grow in living room conditions as it demands constant warmth and humidity.

Temperatures:
Growing season	15–24 °C	(60–75 °F)
Minimum winter	15 °C	(60 °F)

Soil: A soil-less compost.

Where it likes to be: In the lightest position possible, protected from sun.

What it likes to drink: Tepid water. Ensure that the soil stays moist. It is a high humidity plant; see page 5. Mist-spray daily in hot weather, twice weekly at other times, using tepid water.

Making it sensational: Little feeding necessary; very weak liquid feed once or twice in the growing season. Maintain warmth and humidity. As it ages, the leaves will tend to drop. When this occurs, cut it back to one-third of its original height. Tend carefully and new shoots will form.

Giving it a rest: No marked resting period—no special routine.

When it looks sick:
Leaves droop and may drop: You are probably using too much water which is too cold.
Leaves get dry brown borders: Mist-spray regularly and increase the humidity. See page 5.
Plant loses colour: It needs better light, though not full sun.
Leaves droop: Check that soil is moist. If not, water to correct condition.

Coleus

FLAME NETTLE

These are highly ornamental plants of orderly growth, valued for their foliage. The leaves are shaped like those of the common stinging nettle but are so varied in colours and combinations of colours that two are seldom alike. The flowers are insignificant and should be removed to make the plant stronger. Given a liberal diet and plenty of light, they are among the easiest of all indoor plants to grow and maintain.

Coleus is a good plant to group with others.

Temperatures:
Growing season   20-24°C   (68-75°F)
Minimum winter   15°C   (60°F)

Soil: A soil-less compost.

44

Where it likes to be: A south-facing sunny position summer and winter, protected from hot sunshine. It is not susceptible to draughts or temperature changes.

What it likes to drink: Enough tepid water to keep the soil moist, possibly twice daily for large plants. Avoid leaves. No spraying needs.

Making it sensational: Feed once a week. Pinch out growing tips to produce a good bushy shape. Remove flowers that appear. Cut off dead or damaged leaves, using a sloping cut, and lightly dust the wound with fungicide powder.

Giving it a rest: It doesn't usually survive its rest period. Coleus is cheap and grows quickly. Buy another.

When it looks sick:
Leaves flag: Caused by over or under-watering. Check soil conditions. Too warm an atmosphere causes leaves to lose moisture faster than the roots can take it up. If the soil condition is correct, this is almost certainly the reason.
Mildew: This may affect open wounds and the treatment is to dust with fungicide powder.
The plant grows spindly: Pinch out the tips to force a lusher growth and stand the plant in better light.
Stained and blotchy leaves: Stop allowing water to get onto the leaves. Check regularly for pests. Mealy bug is a possibility. See page 6.

Fuchsia

FUCHSIA

The plants are available in a great variety of colours, with single or double flowers. Standards (tree-shaped, on a single tall stem) or well-shaped little bushes, they may be trained into pyramids by pinching out in early stages of growth. Some varieties trail attractively and may be hung from rafters. They are easy, trouble-free plants to grow. The popular Fuchsias all have dainty dark green foliage and a profusion of graceful pendant blooms.

Temperatures:

Growing season	12–15 °C	(53–60 °F)
Minimum winter (frost-free vital)	7 °C	(45 °F)
Rest period (maximum)	10 °C	(50 °F)

Soil: A soil-less or John Innes No 2 compost.

Where it likes to be: In a light, airy position sheltered from strong sun. They are not specially sensitive to draughts or moderate changes in temperature.

What it likes to drink: Water to maintain a moist soil condition. When growing strongly, this is a thirsty plant, but it should not be drowned. There are no spraying or humidity requirements.

Making it sensational: Fuchsias may be trained or grown into many shapes. Feed weekly with weak liquid fertilizer from bud formation to end of flowering. Remove faded blooms to ensure a succession of flowers.

Giving it a rest: When flowering ends, steadily reduce water until the soil is only slightly moist. Place in a cool, frost-free spot for the winter. In spring, give more light and slowly stage back to normal watering and temperature. When the buds begin to swell, cut back the stems, leaving three or four buds on each. As the plant develops, pinch out as necessary to produce required shape.

When it looks sick:
Buds and/or leaves drop: It may be too warm; place it in a cooler spot. Another cause may be overwatering. It needs plenty of water when growing vigorously in warm weather but little and often is the rule.
The leaves droop and the plant has a tired appearance: Probably caused by under-watering. Restore moist soil condition.
Insects : Check regularly. Treat as shown on page 6.

Pelargonium zonale, Pelargonium regale

GERANIUM

Zonal Pelargoniums are the 'Geraniums' which are deservedly popular for use indoors and out. They have round leaves with scalloped edges and horse-shoe shaped markings. They blossom prolifically in a great range of shades from white through scarlet. The colours are brilliant.

Regal Pelargoniums have large petals, but flower less freely once the first generous flush is over. They make well shaped plants and their range of fine colours and combinations is immense. They are true indoor plants.

Temperatures:
Growing season   12 °C (53 °F) upwards
Minimum winter (Frost-free)   4 °C   (39 °F)

Soil: Add 25% good friable garden loam to soil-less compost. They prefer a porous calcareous compost which must be well-drained.

Where it likes to be: In a bright sunny spot, with good ventilation, the <u>Zonal Geranium</u> can stand draughts and temperature fluctuations if it must. The <u>Regal Pelargonium</u> likes warmth and shelter, is less tolerant and more sensitive to strong sun.

What it likes to drink: Tepid tap water. Spraying and special humidity are unnecessary.

Making it sensational: Maintain moist soil condition, springy to the thumb. They can stand a period of dryness but will be seriously harmed if over-watered. Feed fortnightly with well-diluted liquid fertilizer. When re-potting add a teaspoonful of bone meal to the compost. Pinch out to induce a good bushy shape; stop removing shoots once they are well branched. <u>Regals</u> require less pinching. Remove faded blooms.

Giving it a rest. Most people start new plants from cuttings. To over-winter, reduce water until the soil is almost dry. Stand plants in cool, airy frost-free place. In spring, cut back, re-pot. Slowly stage up watering as growth increases and give plenty of light and ventilation. Pinch out for shape.

When it looks sick:
Lush, leafy growth but few blooms: Over-feeding causes this. Stop feeding and, in the case of <u>Zonals</u>, pinch out the tips to encourage branching and bud formation.
Aphids : Spray as shown on page 6.
Other symptoms : See *P. peltata*, a closely related plant.

Sinningia Hybrids

GLOXINIA

One of the most beautiful and sensational of house-plants. Clusters of large, velvety, trumpet-shaped flowers surmount beautiful foliage in this low growing plant. A vast range of very pure colours is available.

Temperatures:
Growing season	22–24 °C (72–75 °F)
Minimum winter	Store tubers in dry frost-free place.

Soil: A soil-less compost or John Innes No 2 with 30 % sphagnum peat.

Where it likes to be: In plenty of light but protected from sun and draughts.

What it likes to drink: Lukewarm water daily to keep soil moist in growing period. Avoid water on leaves or flowers. Mist-spray daily in hot weather when not in flower. Avoid droplets on leaves—shake them off. It likes humidity—see page 5.

Making it sensational: Give weak liquid fertilizer once every week. Carefully cut off faded blooms and damaged leaves; dust any open wounds lightly with a powder fungicide.

Giving it a rest: After flowering, stop water and feeding; let it die down completely. Dust with fungicide powder and place in dark, frost-free spot until spring. In late April, re-pot the tubers in fresh compost and in a <u>clean</u> pot. Place in a warm position and water lightly. When growth starts, increase water and begin slowly to feed. Keep water away from the crown of the plant.

When it looks sick:
Leaves limp and dull, the flower trumpets tending to collapse: Check the soil; if dry, water and spray. If the soil is moist, spray the plant and improve humidity—see page 5.
Leaves firm but lacking a healthy deep green gloss : May be aphids—treat as shown on page 6.
Rotting spots on leaves: Caused by water droplets after watering or spraying. Dust affected areas lightly with fungicidal powder.

Rhoicissus rhomboidea

GRAPE IVY

A very popular, vigorous climbing plant which does well in most situations and is particularly good where light is limited. It does need support to look its best, and a trellis is ideal.

Temperatures:

Growing season	15-21°C	(60-70°F)
Minimum winter	13°C	(55°F)

Soil: A soil-less compost.

Where it likes to be: This plant must not be positioned in full sunlight, and can tolerate fairly low light.

What it likes to drink: Check the soil carefully before watering as it only likes to be slightly moist and over-watering will kill the plant quickly. Spray twice a week in summer.

Making it sensational: Train the plant over a trellis or support of some kind and pinch back to maintain a bushy habit.

Giving it a rest: Growth slows in winter so less water is needed. Keep the compost just moist.

When it looks sick:
Leaves droop and fall: Either too cold or the plant has been over-watered. Allow to dry out then check the soil condition before each watering.
Leaves turn brown and fall: A few lower leaves will fall under normal circumstances. If a number of leaves fall, move to a cooler place, water and spray more frequently.
Leaves turn pale and growth slows: The plant may need feeding or re-potting.
Insect pests : Identify from page 6 and treat as instructed.

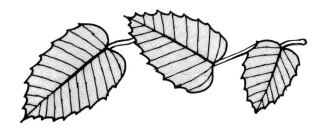

Hedera helix, Hedera canariensis

IVY

There is a wide variety of ornamental ivies. They are attractive climbing plants with variegated or glossy green leaves. Most are quite hardy and easy to care for, but a few need specialized care. Follow the instructions given on the plant label.

Ivies combine excellently with other foliage plants and are very tolerant of variable light and temperature conditions. *H. canariensis* will achieve magnificent proportions if re-potted when necessary.

Temperatures:

Growing season	10-18°C	(50-64°F)
Minimum winter	Frost free	

Soil: A soil-less or John Innes No 2 compost.

Where it likes to be: In a light sun-free position. *H. helix* tolerates some draughts and temperature changes, but the variety *H. canariensis* is more delicate.

What it likes to drink: Tepid water. Keep soil moist and springy—only just moist in winter. Spray weekly in hot weather.

Making it sensational: Feed at two or three week intervals with weak fertilizer. Avoid over-feeding or the plant may become too lush. Ivy hangs, trails and climbs well and is at its best in the company of contrasting foliage plants.

Giving it a rest: No marked rest period; no special routine. Guard against over-watering, especially in cold weather.

When it looks sick:
Dry browned leaves : Sunscorch or too high temperature. Move it to a less sunny spot. It could also be under-watering. Check soil condition; keep it moist.
Leaves flag and tend to fall: Almost certainly over-watering. Allow plant to dry out and then water to keep a moist soil condition.
Aphids and scale insects : See page 6.

Fatshedera

IVY TREE, CLIMBING FIG LEAF PALM

A vigorous house plant capable of considerable growth. The variegated varieties require a slightly higher temperature. The species, *lizei*, is probably the most popular.

Temperatures:

Growing season	15 °C	(60 °F)
Minimum winter	4–7 °C	(39–45 °F)

Soil: A soil-less or John Innes No 2 compost.

Where it likes to be: Place in a light non-sunny position. The plant is tolerant of draughts and temperature changes.

What it likes to drink: Lukewarm water. Always maintain a moist soil condition and water on the soil. No spraying is necessary, nor does the plant demand high humidity.

Making it sensational: Feed weekly with weak liquid fertilizer. Cut back in spring for a bushier plant. No pinching out, except for shaping. If it has been in the same pot for a long time and looks tired, re-pot in fresh compost. It will not thrive in too high a temperature.

Giving it a rest: There is no marked resting period.

When it looks sick:
Leaves tend to flag and become pale : Reduce watering, as this is the most likely cause.
Growth too lush and soft : Stop feeding.
Damaged, browning leaves and a tendency to wilt : Reposition out of sunlight.
Aphids : See page 6.

Cissus antarctica

KANGAROO VINE

A useful, fast-growing vine that will quickly cover a wall, room divider or trellis. It is a true climber, supporting itself by tendrils. The long, heart-shaped leaves with toothed edges are a clear shade of green. In shops and offices it can often be seen, the sole survivor in a container once filled with plants. It will fight to live, even in the most unfavourable, dark places.

Temperatures:

Growing season	15–24 °C	(60–75 °F)
Minimum winter	7–10 °C	(45–50 °F)

Soil: A soil-less or John Innes No 2 compost.

Where it likes to be: It tolerates quite a lot of shade but thrives in good light. Do not expose it to hot sun. It can stand wide temperature changes and is fairly tolerant of draughts, but dislikes hot, dry air.

What it likes to drink: In the growing season, it is a copious drinker and will need frequent watering. Mist-spray when the air is dry—daily in summer. At other times, spray and gently wipe leaves when they look dusty. The plant likes humidity. See page 5.

Making it sensational: Give a very weak liquid feed every two to four weeks depending on growth rate. Too much encouragement and it will take over the house. Do not hesitate to cut back.

Giving it a rest: It never appears to rest and no action is necessary.

When it looks sick:
Leaves drop: Improve humidity and cut out unsightly stems once the plant shows signs of recovery.
Leaves crinkle and drop: It is too cold. Place it in an even temperature.
The plant grows lush and invasive: Stop feeding and cut back to a more satisfactory size. Cut at a leaf joint.
Yellowing leaves: Too much light; give it some shade. When bought, this plant may be in too small a pot. Give it four to six weeks to settle before re-potting. Do not over-pot since it will grow very big quite quickly.

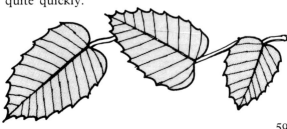

Adiantum

MAIDENHAIR FERN

There are many species of Maidenhair Fern and all
are dainty, beautiful plants. Good varieties are *cunea-
tum decorum* and *williamsii*. The foliage of tiny, clear
green leaves, often heart-shaped, held on fine delicate
stems, and cascading over the sides of the pot, make
this fern the perfect foil for other plants.

Temperatures:

Growing season	12–15 °C	(53–60 °F)
Minimum winter	7 °C	(45 °F)

They do not like too high a temperature!

Soil: A soil-less compost.

Where it likes to be: In a light shady position, protected from sunlight. Keep out of draughts and avoid wide temperature changes.

What it likes to drink: Rainwater, to maintain a moist soil condition. Good drainage is essential. The soil must never dry out since this will damage the root hairs. Ferns like very humid atmosphere—see page 24. Spray regularly with a fine syringe in hot weather.

Making it sensational: Feed weekly during the growing season with well-diluted 'Baby Bio' or other plant food.

Giving it a rest: There is no marked resting period, and no special routine needed. If re-potting, do not disturb the soil ball. Simply slide it into a slightly larger pot, which is well drained, and top up with new compost, to which a little crushed charcoal should be added in order to keep it sweet. Completely bury the old soil.

When it looks sick:
Wilting fronds: Increase humidity by spraying and by improving environment. Ferns prefer a moist atmosphere in a light shade.
Wilting fronds and yellowing leaves: Stop feeding. If the soil is dry, water generously with soft water but good drainage must exist.
Brown scorched leaflets: Take the plant out of the sunlight which probably caused the complaint. Cut off badly affected fronds close to their bases.

Maranta leuconeura

MARANTA, PRAYER PLANT

These compact plants have large oval leaves and are grown for their ornamental foliage. *Var : kerchoreana* has midgreen smooth leaves with about ten purple markings on the upper surface which give it the common name Rabbit's Tracks. (Underneath, the leaves are a muted purple in colour.) Another variety, *erythrophylla* has bright red veins on leaves which are bright green along the central rib. The common name, Prayer Plant, is derived from the leaves' habit of folding up together at night.

Temperatures:

Growing season	18-22°C	(64-72°F)
Minimum winter	10°C	(50°F)

Soil: A soil-less or John Innes No 2 compost.

Where it likes to be: In light shade and out of direct sunlight. It is moderately tolerant but draughts or excessive temperature fluctuations can result in unsightly leaf damage.

What it likes to drink: Maintain a moist soil condition with lukewarm soft water. It likes high humidity; see page 5. Mist-spray daily in hot weather; weekly at other times.

Making it sensational: Maintain humidity and spray daily in hot weather. Cut off damaged leaves with brown tips. Give a well-diluted liquid fertilizer weekly in spring, summer and autumn, but not in winter. Re-pot into a shallow pot in spring using fresh compost and ensure good drainage.

Giving it a rest: Maintain a moist soil condition in winter. No special routine; the rest period is only a slowing of growth in cold weather.

When it looks sick:
Plant seems loose in the soil and looks tired and sick: Root-rot caused by over-watering. Try re-potting; the plant may not survive but will die if left.
Leaves drying and going brown and dry: Probably under-watered; use soft, lukewarm water to restore soil condition.
Browning tips and edges to leaves: Check the humidity as this is the probable cause. Spray regularly in warm weather.

Sansevieria trifasciata laurentii

MOTHER-IN-LAW'S TONGUE

A tall, spiky plant which looks like a cactus or succulent, but is actually of the Lily family. The thick
spear-like leaves can reach a considerable height and
are very erect. They are variegated, pale and darker
green. *Var. laurentii* also includes cream in its pat-
terning. The flowers are insignificant.

Temperatures:
    Growing season   16–21 °C (61–70 °F)
    Temperature should be constant throughout the
    year. The plant cannot stand wide temperature
    changes.

Soil: A soil-less compost, with 10% added sand.

Where it likes to be: In a light position out of direct sunlight, away from draughts and temperature changes.

What it likes to drink: Lukewarm water to keep the soil just moist. Excessive water in winter is disastrous; the leaves rot at soil level and the plant dies. No spraying or humidity needed.

Making it sensational: If it tries to flower, pinch out the flowering stem, as it weakens the plant. Give a very dilute liquid fertilizer once monthly. Never risk over watering—in winter it needs only just enough to stop total drying out. Do not over-pot. Re-pot only when the plant forces it way out. Maintain an even temperature.

Giving it a rest: There is no clearly defined rest period.

When it looks sick:
Brown, striated areas along the leaf edges: Scorch by strong sunlight. They may also be due to under-watering. Keep it in light shade; water if the soil is dry.

The commonest cause of death has no symptom. Over-watering causes the leaves to rot below the soil surface. Never, never over-water this plant.

Chamaedorea elegans

PARLOUR PALM

Also know as Neanthe bella, the Parlour Palm has attractive long spiky leaves. It likes a position away from direct sunlight, and is fairly easy to care for as long as the soil is always kept moist.

Temperatures:

Growing season	16-18°C	(60-65°F)
Minimum winter	13°C	(55°F)

Soil: A mixture of 30% peat and 70% soil-less compost.

Where it likes to be: In reasonable light but away from direct sunlight. It will tolerate a dark position but will grow very slowly.

What it likes to drink: The soil must be kept moist and springy and not be allowed to dry out, so water regularly. Wipe the leaves each week to keep dust-free and increase humidity.

Making it sensational: Feed during the summer about every fourteen days.

Giving it a rest: Reduce water in winter, but maintain the soil in a moist condition.

When it looks sick:
Tips of leaves turn brown: Move out of direct sunlight to a cooler place and water.
Insect pests: Identify from page 6 and treat as instructed.
Leaves rot and fall off: Temperature is too low, and the plant may have been over-watered. Move to a warmer place and allow to dry out.

Aloe variegata

PARTRIDGE BREASTED ALOE

Striking rosette-shaped succulent plants with thick spear-shaped leaves. The leaves are broadly striped from side to side with bands of olive green and white and have a narrow white edge. They do not demand a lot of attention.

Temperature:
Minimum all year   10 °C   (50 °C)

Soil: A soil-less compost mixed with 20% sharp sand.

Where it likes to be: In summer, it dislikes full sun. In winter, keep in a light frost-free position.

What it likes to drink: Keep soil moist, rather less so in winter. Succulents can survive under-watering to a high degree. Spraying and humidity are unnecessary.

Making it sensational: They need feeding with weak liquid fertilizer only two or three times per season.

Giving it a rest: In winter growth slows; less water is needed. Place in light, frost-free, sheltered position.

When it looks sick:

Browned edges to sections of the leaves: This is usually caused by a combination of mistreatments. Harsh sunlight through glass coupled with gross under-watering may cause it. Widely fluctuating temperatures, coupled with draughts and gross under-watering have an identical effect.

The plant is rocky and loose in the soil: Stop over-watering. Allow the soil to dry out and then water sparingly. The looseness is the result of root-rot weakening the plant's hold in sodden soil.

Peperomia caperata

PEPPER ELDER

A very dainty little plant with deeply crinkled leaves and erect catkin-like cream flowers. The leaves are a very deep green, and the plant has a domed compact shape. There are a number of different varieties of Peperomia and all make charming house plants which mix well with other foliage plants.

Peperomia sandersii has cupped oval pointed leaves which are a bluish-green striped with silver.

Peperomia ornata has deeply corrugated leaves with red veins.

Temperatures:

Growing season	15–22 °C	(60–72 °F)
Minimum winter	7 °C	(45 °C)

Soil: A well-drained soil-less compost.

Where it likes to be: In a light position out of sunlight. It will stand a good deal of shade.

What it likes to drink: Lukewarm rainwater applied under the leaves to keep the soil springy to thumb pressure. It <u>does not</u> like to be immersed in water. Spray daily in very hot summer weather, once weekly at other times; in winter only occasionally on milder days. It likes humidity; see page 5.

Making it sensational: Plant in a shallow dish. If it is in a group, provide a pocket of broken crocks under it. Feed a very weak liquid fertilizer weekly. Cut off damaged or broken leaves and stems and dead flowers as low as possible. Always use a sloping cut to avoid water retention which encourages rot.

Giving it a rest: No marked rest period. Re-pot in spring if it is cramped.

When it looks sick:
The stems flag, letting the leaves droop: Caused by under-watering or too dry an atmosphere. Water the plant, mist-spray it and improve the humidity.
Poor colour variegation: This improves if you give the plant more light but not full sun.
Insect pests : Identify from page 6 and treat as instructed.

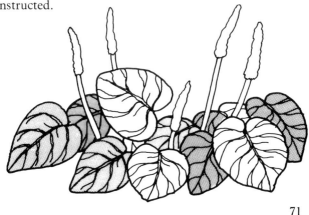

Euphorbia pulcherrima

POINSETTIA

A handsome plant with large dark green leaves of distinctive shape. The flowers are insignificant but are surrounded by large showy bracts of pink, white or scarlet. If the plant is healthy the bracts will last for some weeks. When they finally fade, leaf drop will shortly follow. The plant is not dead, but as it is deciduous it is simply beginning its period of rest. With care it may be re-started in the right season.

Temperatures:

Growing season	15-22°C	(60-72°F)
Minimum	13°C	(55°F)

Soil: A soil-less compost.

Where it likes to be: In light shade in summer; in a bright spot in winter. Draughts or temperature changes cause leaf drop.

What it likes to drink: Keep soil moist and springy to thumb pressure. Tepid soft or rain water is essential as cold water will shock the plant into losing its leaves. It benefits from high humidity—see page 5. Spraying is unnecessary.

Making it sensational: It is not an easy plant to grow; it needs careful watering, good drainage and a fortnightly feed of weak liquid fertilizer, and dislikes fumes of any kind.

Giving it a rest: The rest period begins after the scarlet bracts fall and the leaves drop. Reduce water gradually until the plant is almost dry. Place it in frost-free cupboard until May, providing only enough water to stop the soil becoming dry and hard. In May, remove it from its pot, cut it down to about 4 ins of stem, shake off the old compost and re-pot it with fresh. Place in a warm, bright spot and slowly increase watering as growth re-starts. Pinch out all but two or three new shoots, keeping those which help the shaping of the plant.

When it looks sick:
The plant loses its leaves: This symptom can follow any incorrect handling of the plant. Check for draughts and sharp temperature drops; move accordingly. Check watering; reduce or increase to restore good moist springy soil condition with lukewarm water. Ensure that it has high humidity; see page 5. If the leaves do fall, the plant is not dead. See 'Giving it a rest'.
Parasites : See page 6.

Hypoestes sanguinolenta

POLKA DOT PLANT

This attractive plant is mainly grown for its unusual foliage, although mature plants do have a delicate purple and white flower. The fine, rounded leaves appear to be dotted with pale pink spots, hence the common name 'polka dot plant'. It is also sometimes know as 'freckle face'. As they are most attractive when young, new plants are generally cultivated each year.

Temperatures:

Growing season	18-21°C	(65-70°F)
Minimum winter	10°C	(50°F)

Soil: A soil-less compost.

Where it likes to be: In a light position, but protected from direct sun. The atmosphere should be fairly humid with good ventilation but no draughts.

What it likes to drink: Tepid water. Keep the soil fairly moist. Humidity is essential, so keep the plant on a saucer of wet pebbles (see page 5).

Making it sensational: Keep in a clean atmosphere, away from fumes, and maintain the humidity. Feed about every fourteen days during the summer.

Giving it a rest: These plants are best when young, so it is usual to take cuttings in early spring.

When it looks sick:
Drooping leaves: May be too cold. Move to a warmer place. It could also be over-watering. Check the soil condition and keep it moist but not too wet.
Scale insects: See page 6.

Ficus Elastica var: decora

RUBBER PLANT

Probably one of the best known foliage plants. It grows very erect, with large leaves, and looks well standing alone or in company with other foliage plants.

Temperatures:

Growing season	15-20°C	(60-68°F)
Minimum winter	10°C	(50°F)

Soil: John Innes No 2 or 3 compost.

Where it likes to be: In a light position away from sun and draughts. Excessive cold will cause the leaves to fall.

What it likes to drink: Keep soil moist to thumb pressure, with lukewarm water—cold can be fatal; avoid leaves. Let the soil dry a little between watering. It needs no spraying but likes some humidity. Feed once a week with a weak liquid fertilizer in its water. Good drainage is essential.

Making it sensational: Sponge leaves to remove dust. Buy special plant polish from the florist to make the leaves shine—it will not harm the plant.

Giving it a rest: No marked rest period and no special routine, but it needs less water and feeding in winter.

When it looks sick:
Leaves begin to drop: This may be due to under- or over-watering. Restore a moist soil condition, with soft, lukewarm water. It may be potbound. Re-pot if necessary.
Leaves drop: It could be the soil condition, draughts or sharp drops in temperature. These should be checked and corrected.
The red stems pale to a dull pink: Stop feeding at once.
Insects : Check regularly for scale insects: see page 6.

Beloperone guttata

SHRIMP PLANT

This showy plant is a native of Mexico. It has oval,
pointed, soft green leaves. The flowers are hidden
amongst distinctive clusters of drooping shrimp pink
bracts which overlap closely and appear at the ends
of the shoots. The plant may not flower for two or
three years, until it is mature, but when it does, the
bracts will persist for most of the summer.

Temperatures:
Growing season	15–22 °C	(60–72 °F)
Minimum winter	10 °C	(50 °F)

Soil: A soil-less or John Innes No 2 compost.

Where it likes to be: A good bright position, protected from strong sunlight. It tolerates slight draughts or temperature changes.

What it likes to drink: Maintain a moist, springy soil condition. No spraying or special humidity conditions are necessary.

Making it sensational: The striking shrimp-like bracts last most of the summer; good light improves the colour. Some leaves may drop in winter. Remove the first bracts to induce more leaves and eventually a larger number bracts. Feed weak liquid fertilizer once monthly.

Giving it a rest: The plant rests in winter. Cease feeding, and reduce water. Keep soil just moist. Move to a cooler, frost-free position. In spring, repot, cut back as necessary, increase warmth and light until growth is vigorous. Increase watering, begin to feed.

When it looks sick:
Leaves drop: Reduce watering.
Leaves become limp and dull: Under-watering is the most likely cause.
The plant appears to be drying: The likely cause is root-rot due to waterlogging. It is difficult to rectify and re-potting is a chance worth taking. Then stand the plant in sheltered shade and it may recover.
Curling leaves: Parasite attack. Inspect plant and when found, deal with them as set out on page 6.

Calceolaria

SLIPPER PLANT

A vivid, showy flowering plant and a favourite as a Mother's Day gift. Large pouch-shaped flowers in reds, yellows, and orange are borne in great clusters over broad bright green leaves. The flowers are always speckled and there is both a small and large flowered variety.

Temperatures:

Flowering season	12-18°C	(53-64°F)
Minimum	8°C	(46°F)

Soil: They are not usually re-potted. Sow in soil-less or John Innes No 1 compost.

Where it likes to be: Likes a good light, cool position but avoid full sunlight. It will droop if placed in a draughty spot.

What it likes to drink: Never allow soil to dry out. The plant likes humidity; without it the leaves may flag. In warm weather, use a fine spray on leaves only.

Making it sensational: These plants are usually bought in flower so feeding is unnecessary. It may be kept and rested in winter but is seldom worth saving. It has been included in this book because the plant is so often given as a gift and rewards the little care that it needs.

Giving it a rest: Treat as an annual and discard after it has finished flowering.

When it looks sick:
Leaves and flowers droop: Probably insufficient water, maintain a moist soil condition. Draughts may affect this plant in a similar way. If the soil condition is good, move the plant to a more sheltered place.
The plant loses its freshness and looks tired: Move it from direct sunlight which is the most probable cause.
Blotchy, unsightly leaves: Check for aphid attack. Too warm a position increases this risk.
Fungus attack can occur: Dust with a fungicidal powder.

Chlorophytum comosum

SPIDER PLANT

This easy plant has grass-like leaves with a white centre stripe and clear green edges. Small plantlets produced at the ends of long arching stems make it suitable for wall display or hanging baskets.

Temperatures:

Growing season	15–22 °C	(60–72 °F)
Minimum winter	7–10 °C	(45–50 °F)

Soil: A soil-less or John Innes No 2 compost.

Where it likes to be: A very light position. Direct sun will cause the leaf tips to dry. It resists draughts and temperature changes.

What it likes to drink: Always keep soil moist and springy to thumb pressure. It is thirsty and needs frequent watering if the weather is hot or the plant big. Needs no special humidity treatment or spraying.

Making it sensational: See that it has adequate room to grow, as stems bearing the young plantlets are not supple. The insignificant flowers should not be removed until dead. Feed weekly with diluted liquid fertilizer while growing. Before it becomes too big and coarse, pot up two or three of the plantlets; they root easily and will replace the mother plant once they are growing steadily. No other treatment is necessary.

Giving it a rest: No obvious rest period. Growth slows as light and warmth reduce in winter. Less water will be needed to maintain the soil condition. In winter feed at four-weekly intervals.

When it looks sick:
The leaf tips go brown and dry: This may be over-watering or shortage of food. It could also be the result of sun scorch. If the soil condition is good, move the plant to a less sunny window.
The leaf tips brown and the plant begins to look unkempt: Re-pot; it has probably outgrown its existing one.

Philodendron scandens

SWEETHEART VINE

A prolific climber when conditions are right. Usually
it has dark green, glossy, heart-shaped leaves, but
other variations are available. The plants are evergreen and are best trained up moss-covered supports
as they produce aerial roots. They usually live quite
happily in a living room and are seen at their best
when mixed with other foliage plants.

Temperatures:
Growing season	15–22 °C	(60–72 °F)
Minimum winter	13 °C	(55 °F)

Soil: John Innes No 2 or 3 compost.

Where it likes to be: It can manage on minimal light, but some sunlight is beneficial in winter. Always protect from hot summer sun.

What it likes to drink: Soft or rainwater to keep the soil moist and springy to thumb pressure. Avoid water on leaves. It is a high humidity plant—see page 5. Spray daily in hot dry weather, weekly at other times but <u>never</u> in cold weather.

Making it sensational: Being a fast growing climber, it needs something to climb on like string or trellis; but cane rods wrapped in moss for the aerial roots to grip are much better and look more attractive. To restrain growth, pinch off top shoots, forcing it to branch. Plants are often sold under-potted, so a transfer to a larger pot and richer compost will be beneficial. After re-potting, maintain soil moisture with just tepid water for a couple of months, then give well-diluted liquid fertilizer weekly.

Giving it a rest: No marked rest period; no special routine.

When it looks sick:
Flagging and curling leaves and weak, soft stems: Check soil condition and if dry, water the plant. The same condition may result from over-watering or over-feeding. In each case cease to do either, resuming watering only when the soil condition has been corrected.
The same symptom may occur even though the watering has been corrected and the plant not overfed: This indicates that it needs re-potting in a larger pot.
A tired, dusty appearance: Insufficient spraying. Increase this and the plant will respond.

Monstera deliciosa

SWISS CHEESE PLANT

An evergreen which can be grown to a considerable
size, it forms an impressive, long-lived plant. The
large, shiny leaves are deeply incised. It produces
aerial roots and should be trained against supports
covered in damp moss, to which the roots can cling.

Temperatures:

Growing season	18-24°C	(64-75°F)
Minimum winter	10°C	(50°F)

Soil: A soil-less or John Innes No 2 compost.

Where it likes to be: It requires a light sunless position, chosen with care; it grows to suit its site and may not shift easily. It is wise to avoid draughts and temperature changes.

What it likes to drink: The soil must always be moist and springy to the touch. It is a big drinker and needs tepid, soft water and daily spraying in hot weather. Provide humidity; see page 5.

Making it sensational: Dry soil or air causes leaf edges to brown. Give well-diluted liquid fertilizer once weekly. It will grow quite large, and a stake or moss pole should be provided for its support. Sponge leaves gently to remove dust, or polish them with one of the special emulsions for that purpose. Re-pot the plant when it becomes totally pot-bound.

Giving it a rest: No marked rest period but growth slows in colder weather. Feeding should be stopped and water reduced to maintain soil condition. Spray with lukewarm water every two or three days at this time.

When it looks sick:
Damaged and tired looking leaves: Too dry an atmosphere or draughts may cause this. Improve humidity; see page 5. Ensure that its position is draught-free.
Leaves drying and becoming brown: The cause is likely to be under-watering. Do not drown it. but restore a moist springy soil condition.
Attack by scale insects: Deal with as shown on page 6.

Cyperus diffusus

UMBRELLA PLANT

No indoor plant is easier to grow than the Umbrella Plant. A good specimen of the variety *C. alternifolius* resembles a graceful group of miniature palm trees and looks elegant on its own or grouped with other plants.

C. diffusus is lower growing and has broader leaves. It is less delicate in looks than *C. alternifolius* but it, too, is an attractive, useful and tolerant plant.

Temperatures:

Growing season	Anywhere between
Minimum winter	10–25 °C (50–77 °F)

Soil: A soil-less compost, though most open-textured soils will suit it.

Where it likes to be: It will thrive in light or shady conditions. It is tough and not sensitive to draughts or temperature changes.

What it likes to drink: Water copiously. Keep soil almost <u>wet</u>. Leave water in the plant saucer. It is a relative of the Egyptian Papyrus—a swamp plant. Very few plants like their roots permanently in water—this one does.

Making it sensational: Feed it fortnightly with weak liquid fertilizer. Re-pot if necessary because of fast growth. The plant may be divided if it gets too big.

Giving it a rest: No special routine. Growth merely slows in winter.

When it looks sick:
The plant looks tired or the leaf tips go brown: Water copiously. You cannot over-water this plant.
Leaves become unsightly or cause the plant to have a bad shape: Clip off the offending leaves near the crown of the plant. They will be replaced quickly.

Aechmea fasciata

URN PLANT

A large, very showy Bromeliad with grey-green leaves arranged in the shape of a funnel. It produces a single large flower that looks as if it were made out of pink wood shavings. Each plant flowers only once, then continues as a foliage plant and can easily be propagated from the small plantlets that grow from its base. It needs a potting compost consisting of coarse peat, sphagnum moss, sterilized leaf mould and some grit.

Temperatures:

Growing season	22–24 °C	(72–75 °F)
Minimum winter	15 °C	(60 °C)

Soil: A potting compost consisting of coarse peat, sphagnum moss, sterilized leaf mould and some grit.

Where it likes to be: In a light position but protected from direct sunlight, which will scorch the leaves. Keep away from draughts.

What it likes to drink: Generous quantities of luke-warm water in summer. Keep the leaf funnel well filled, the soil only just moist. It is a dry air plant and does not need humidity. In very hot weather, however, give a mist spray every two weeks or so.

Making it sensational: In the active growth period give well-diluted liquid fertilizer every two weeks. Cut off flower after it fades. Guard against leaf damage which can be caused by direct sunlight.

Giving it a rest: The plant rests after flowering and will not flower again. No special treatment is needed but it does appreciate winter sunlight. The parent plant will probably die. Propagate from the plantlets which will grow at its base.

When it looks sick:
The plant flags: Mist-spray often and ensure high humidity.
The plant leans in its pot: Firm down the soil. Water with soft water in strict moderation. Ensure good drainage or root-rot will swiftly give trouble.
Yellowing or pale-looking leaves: Stop feeding at once.

Yucca elephantipes

YUCCA

A very popular plant for the house or conservatory with clusters of long, spiky leaves. They are easy to care for if given plenty of light.

Temperatures:
Growing season	12°C (55°F) upwards
Minimum winter	7°C (45°F)

Soil: A soil-less compost.

Where it likes to be: In a bright sunny spot, with good humidity. They do not like to be too hot and dry in the summer, and can be put outside in a sunny spot on a patio.

What it likes to drink: Keep the soil moist, watering frequently in the summer months. Spray each week.

Making it sensational: Feed half the recommended dose of liquid fertilizer every week during the summer. Keep the leaves clean and dust-free by wiping with a damp cloth.

Giving it a rest: Growth slows in the winter, so only water about every ten days.

When it looks sick:
Yellow leaves: Not enough light. Move to a better position.
Insect pests: Identify from page 6 and treat as instructed.

Aphelandra squarrosa louisae. Var: Silver Queen

ZEBRA PLANT

A very showy plant. It has wide, pointed leaves of a glossy green strongly veined in cream. It is valued for its striking foliage, but also bears a spike of bright yellow flowers.

Temperatures:

Growing season	18–22 °C	(64–72 °C)
Minimum winter	18 °C	(64 °F)

Soil: A soil-less or John Innes No 2 compost kept moist and springy with soft lime-free water.